CLOSE OF PL

Published to coincide with the premiere production at the National Theatre in May 1979, this brilliant black comedy of manners to some extent returns to the territory so wittily explored in *Otherwise Engaged*. *Close of Play* is about a middle-class family reunion, where the sweetness and light intended to accompany such an occasion are progressively eclipsed by revelations of inadequacy, insensitivity and mutual incompatibility. The play contains some of the sharpest writing and most acute character observation to be had in the modern theatre.

The photograph on the back cover is reproduced by courtesy of Beryl Gray.

Simon Gray

CLOSE OF PLAY

EYRE METHUEN . LONDON

First published in 1979 by Eyre Methuen Ltd
11 New Fetter Lane, London EC4P 4EE
Copyright © 1979 by Simon Gray
IBM set in 10 point Journal by 𝔸 Tek-Art, Croydon, Surrey
Printed in Great Britain by Whitstable Litho Ltd
Whitstable, Kent

ISBN 0 413 45840 7 (Paperback)

At the time of going to press, **Close of Play** was scheduled for first performance in the Lyttleton auditorium of the National Theatre in May 1979. The cast was as follows:

JASPER	Sir Michael Redgrave
DAISY	Dame Peggy Ashcroft
HENRY	Michael Gambon
MARIANNE	Anna Massey
BENEDICT	John Standing
MARGARET	Lynn Farleigh
JENNY	
MATTHEW	*Not cast at time of going to press*

Directed by Harold Pinter

Act One

The Curtain rises on the stage in darkness. There is the sound of organ music, at first faint, then swelling until it fills the theatre. As it does so a faint pool of light spreads over JASPER *in his armchair. He appears to be asleep. The music stops mid-chord.* JASPER *opens his eyes, as the rest of the lights come up steadily, until the room is filled with bright summer sunshine.*

Off, left, from beyond the french windows in the garden, the sound of children playing football. HENRY's *voice sounds among theirs.*

DAISY (*comes through on the run, goes to the french windows, calls out*). Henry — Henry dear — will you ask them to keep it right down — right down dear — because of the windows — oh, they can't hear — and as they're going to the Piece later on surely they can wait — and Marianne's forgotten Nindy's pottie again, can you believe, I know what she says about wee-wee being perfectly hygienic and Romans brushing their teeth in it but I don't like her putting her on our soup tureen, do you — but oh Good Heavens Jasper, you've got the lights on, didn't you realise dear, you don't need the lights now it's so light — it's not going to rain for a bit yet you know — (*turning them off*) there — there that's better isn't it, now then, tell me, what did you think of the dumplings, nobody's mentioned them, I was afraid they hadn't thawed right through and I saw your face when you bit into one, you didn't bite into ice, did you dear, I know how you hate cold in your mouth — it goes right through your system I know, is that what happened, did you bite on ice?

JENNY *enters, left, carrying a shopping bag.*

Oh there you are, dear, back already, that was quick.

JENNY. Is Matthew here?

DAISY. What, Matthew, no dear, isn't he with you? He ran after you to catch you up, didn't he Jasper?

JENNY. Oh what a nuisance, I thought I saw him when I came out, on the other side of the street, but the traffic was so appalling it was ages before I could cross and when I did he was gone, so he probably chose to cross to me just as I was crossing to him, and when he found I wasn't there he crossed back just as I was crossing back — why on earth didn't he stay here, as I told him.

DAISY. What dear, well, never mind, you got the muffins did you, that's the main thing. (*Going to take them.*)

JENNY. Oh yes, well I'm afraid I could only get a dozen, Nanty, so I got half a dozen rock-cakes as well, I hope that's all right.

DAISY. What, what do you mean, but I ordered a dozen and a half muffins specially, didn't I Jasper? They promised to keep them, they swore they would, did you say who they were for, did you say they were for Professor Jasper Spencer?

JENNY. Well no, I think I said they were for you, Miss Blightforth —

DAISY. Oh well that explains it, you should have said Professor Jasper Spencer, they know his name in all the shops, don't they Jasper, particularly the baker's, well never mind dear, but rock-cakes you say, I don't know who's going to eat rock-cakes —

JENNY. Matthew loves them, I know.

DAISY. What, Matthew, well of course if Matthew — anyway how much is that I owe you, dear, the muffins are three and a half half p. each I know, at least they were last week and they can't have gone up again in spite of the Common Market, can they Jasper?

JENNY. Oh please, let them be my contribution — as a matter of fact I —

DAISY. What, certainly not. Good Heavens, we wouldn't dream, would we, Jasper, you're our guests you know — so say three and a half p. the muffins, now Matthew's rock-cakes dear, how much were they?

JENNY. Oh four p. I think, but really Nanty —

DAISY. What, four p. Did you hear that, Jasper, four p. Matthew's rock-cakes! So that's three and a half times twelve equals forty-two, now, where's my handbag, the muffins plus six times four equals twenty-four, the rock-cakes, it was on the table, I know! Plus forty-two the muffins comes to sixty-six p. ah here it is sixty-six p. I owe altogether dear. (*Rooting around in her handbag.*) Oh but it's not here, but I'm sure I put it back after the milkman, Jasper do you know what I did with it?

JENNY. Actually Nanty, I do think I'd better get back to the High, you see Matthew's only got today off from school, I have to take him back first thing tomorrow, and as I haven't seen him for quite a while I was rather looking forward to a stroll and a chat with him, to find out how he's getting on and that sort of thing. (*Moving off left.*) So I'll see you later.

DAISY. What, but it was here you know, you know the one Jasper, small, green, in velours, you gave it to me yourself, you know how careful I am —

MARGARET *enters through the arch.*

Oh hello dear, we're just looking for my purse, my small green one in velours — but oh, thank you so much for the dishes.

MARGARET. The dishes?

DAISY. Helping Marianne with them, so sweet of you.

MARGARET. Actually Nanty, I'm afraid I didn't.

DAISY. What, oh then she's had to do them all by herself, oh dear, well — well never mind, she'll have finished them by now almost won't she Jasper, so you come and tell us all your news dear, it's so difficult at lunch isn't it, with all Henry's and Marianne's little ones, and it's such a long time since we've seen you and Benedict, we're dying to hear all about your adventures on that T.V. programme, we saw you, you know, did Jasper tell you, sitting there as cool as a cucumber with a beret on, wasn't it, and the way you talked to that little man with the working-class accent, where was he from, anyway?

MARGARET. Oxford.

DAISY. What, not the University, you don't mean?

MARGARET. Yes. All Souls —

DAISY. Good Heavens, Jasper, did you hear that, the little
working-class man who interviewed Margaret was from Oxford,
aren't you glad you didn't take that Chair after all, well you
certainly put him in his place, dear, asking you all those
questions and paying you those ridiculous compliments, and
you just saying yes and no as if you couldn't be bothered with
him to the manner born, I always say Jasper should have been
on T.V., don't I Jasper, especially now they've got colour,
because of his white mane you know, so distinguished, but I
suppose they're not interested in Latin translations and
mediaeval what-nots dear, you should have been a novelist like
Margaret dear, and you could too, couldn't he Margaret, with
his imagination, not that yours isn't very interesting too dear,
oh yes I've read your novel you know, as soon as I heard you
and Benedict were really coming down at last I went straight
out and borrowed a copy from the library, didn't I Jasper?

BENEDICT *enters through the arch.*

BENEDICT. Oh, you're in here, are you, darling? I've been
waiting for you in the dining-room.

DAISY. Oh well, she's been talking to your father, dear, telling us
all about her success and fame and what have you, you must
be so proud of her, dear.

BENEDICT. What, Nanty?

DAISY. What, dear?

There is a pause.

Proud of her, I mean.

BENEDICT. Oh. Maggie you mean?

DAISY. Yes dear.

BENEDICT. Yes. Yes I am, Nanty. Very proud. (*Little pause.*)
Very proud. Very very proud. Aren't I darling? Um — um —
(*Sits down.*)

DAISY. Are you all right, dear? Is he all right?

BENEDICT. What Nanty?

DAISY. Are you all right, dear? You've been very quiet and grave, you know, all through lunch, and he hardly ate a thing Jasper, did he Margaret, you didn't touch the dumplings didn't you like them?

BENEDICT. Oh. Oh well I'm not very — very keen on food at the moment, am I darling?

DAISY. But you didn't speak either, hardly a word, and look at you now, not at all like your usual self, is he Jasper — but I know — I know what you want to cheer you up, oh how silly of me to have forgotten when I went to all the trouble of remembering to get it in specially, but then it's your fault, it's been such a long time since you came to see us, now where did I put it — oh in the hall — or — anyway Jasper you tell him all our news while I go and find it — I'll be right back dear. (*Going off left.*)

There is a pause.

MARGARET (*goes to* BENEDICT, *sits down beside him*). You're doing marvellously darling.

BENEDICT. What, darling?

MARGARET. Marvellously.

BENEDICT. I feel — I feel —

MARGARET. I can imagine, darling. I can.

BENEDICT (*emotionally*). I know. I know you can. Thank you darling. (*Looks towards* JASPER.) Daddy — I — um — I know I owe you an explanation. For not being in touch for such a long time. The truth is I've been going — going through rather a bad time, haven't I darling? And — and I didn't want to worry you. I expect you can guess what it was. My drinking. Well, not to put too fine a point on it, I wasn't just getting drunk now and then, which is what you must have thought, Daddy, I was actually on my way to becoming an alcoholic, wasn't I darling? So Maggie finally — bless her — put it to me that I had to choose. Between her and my scotch. And she meant it. Didn't you darling? She really meant it. So I — I put myself in the hands of a psychiatrist who had a very good reputation — at least some friends of Maggie's thought very highly of him, didn't they darling — Roger and Liza — but he turned out to be an old-fashioned, rather hard-line Freudian. So as far as he was concerned, I was classic text-book stuff. Went into all my relationships — sibling rivalry of course — you know, that I'd always been jealous of Henry and Dick — Dick particularly, of course, said one of the reasons I drank was because I was guilty because I was glad that Dick was dead and — well, you can imagine — and you, of course, Daddy, which he got down to the old penis envy, naturally, and when I told him I'd never actually seen your penis so how could I envy it, it might be smaller than mine, after all — (*laughs*) well, that was in our first session, believe it or not — eventually he got on to Maggie, of course, said I envied *her* penis, didn't he darling, in the form of her talent, you see — and on top of all his — his clap-trap he was a pretty heavy drinker himself, I could smell alcohol on his breath and — well, by and large he was making things worse not better but of course the trouble was — I did develop a degree of dependence on him and — well, God knows what would have happened to me if I hadn't finally broken free — with the help of, well, Maggie of course, I can't tell you how wonderful — wonderful! she's been — but also of a new chap I happened to hear about at the B.B.C. — Vintross. Norman Vintross. It's because of him that I haven't touched a drop of scotch for what is it, darling, six, no, no, he insists on an absolutely ruthless accounting — it's part of his therapy, five, five weeks Daddy, isn't it darling?

MARGARET. Days, isn't it, darling?

BENEDICT. What?

MARGARET. Days, I think, darling.

BENEDICT. Yes, darling?

MARGARET. Didn't you say weeks.

BENEDICT. Oh, good God, did I really? (*Laughs.*) Days I meant of course, Daddy, six days. But when you think what I was up to — four bottles a day, Daddy.

MARGARET. More like three really, wasn't it darling?

BENEDICT. Oh now darling — well, between three and four — three and a half on a good day, bad day, — that's what Vintross had to contend with, Daddy, so in my view he's a bit of a genius, quite simply. But absolutely practical, that's his great — his great, isn't it darling?

MARGARET. But he does fairly sophisticated things too, doesn't he darling, hypnosis for example.

BENEDICT. God yes, and you should see his eyes when he's putting me under, Daddy — burr — like chips of blue ice, little chips of blue ice, aren't they darling?

MARGARET. Well, I've never met him, don't forget, darling.

BENEDICT. Oh. No, of course you haven't — but what he goes for above all is character, Daddy. In the traditional sense, rather like a Scots school-teacher, eh Maggie, with rewards and punishments and rules and methods. Says I've only one basic problem. I'm weak. Feeble. Gutless. A moral no-hoper. So the only possible solution for types like me is to avoid drink altogether. To stay out of pubs and licensed restaurants — I virtually move with the luncheon voucher set now, Daddy, and he's even shown me a trick for dealing with the B.B.C. parties I can't get out of — he says most of the newsreaders have had to come to him at one time or another — anyway, how to stand — look, legs splayed and hands locked behind my back — (*does it*) to make it difficult to whip a glass from a passing tray or otherwise receive one —

MARGARET (*has got up*). Darling, I think I'll go for a little walk.

BENEDICT. What, on your own, you mean?

MARGARET. Well, I think you and your father should have some time together —

BENEDICT. Oh, well that's all right, isn't it Daddy? Don't go on our account — unless you want to do a bit of creative mulling, of course — did you know Maggie's just begun a new one, Daddy — last week — isn't that marvellous! And I expect she's frightened that I'm going to launch into one of my panegyrics — about what she's meant to me — her support and — (*takes her hand, kisses it*) and in fact you can thank her for our getting down to see you at last, Daddy, she absolutely insisted we come, didn't you, darling — well then, don't be too long — I'll miss you —

MARGARET *goes out through the french windows.*

BENEDICT. Isn't she remarkable, Daddy? Oh, I don't just mean in her talent, although that's remarkable enough God knows

when you think what the odds were against her finishing it. I
mean me, of course, I was the odds. Because you see Daddy —
oh, it sounds so bizarre now but in my worst phase — when I
was adding scotch to my breakfast coffee, you know *that*
stage, — I got it into my head that — well, that she was having
an affair. A real love affair, you see — and what made it more
dreadful, more nightmarish, was that I thought it was with
someone I knew but I didn't know who, if you follow — I knew
I knew the chap, even though there wasn't a chap at all — not
even evidence, Daddy, which of course simply made me more
insane. It got so I started to pick quarrels with friends, people
I work with at the Beeb, interpreting their remarks, their looks,
even — actually even their smells — tried to sniff them, if
they'd been out of their offices a suspiciously long time — and
of course trying to catch poor Maggie in the act, taxi-ing home
at any hour, climbing in through the lavatory window so they
wouldn't hear me in the hall, then up the stairs in my socks,
flinging her study door open after crouching outside it for
hours — and there she'd be, typing calmly away, with her
glasses on, you know she wears glasses for her writing, and of
course the inevitable cigarette hanging from her lips, and she'd
give me such a distracted, absent-minded look, as if for a
second she didn't know who I was, let alone why I was there —
and so — more and more often I'd go well berserk — quite
berserk — and oh God — well the drink, you see, and knowing
she was being unfaithful and not knowing who with but
knowing I knew him and then realizing it was all a delusion —
but now when I think, think of the Hell I put her through,
what she's suffered — endured because of me — well even
Vintross, whose pretty tough about these things was appalled
when I told him — he said — he said that I — I — was a lucky
man to have such an unlucky wife — (*puts his hand to his eyes,
in tears.*) Sorry. Sorry Daddy — but I — I've always loved her
you know but now — now — sorry — I'll be — I'll be all right —
(*Sits, over-come.*)

DAISY (*enters from left, carrying a scotch bottle*). Upstairs — it
was upstairs in my bedroom, in the carrier bag, you see, the
one with the pink wool and the door-knob, anyway I've found
it, that's the thing — (*she is pouring some into a glass*) I got it
in specially for you, because I remembered how you like to

settle down with a nice large one after lunch — there, dear, you keep it beside you so you know where it is — what dear?

BENEDICT (*is staring appalled from the scotch to* DAISY). Nothing. (*Laughs.*) Nothing Nanty that a — a Vintrossian — (*Gets up.*)

DAISY. What, dear?

BENEDICT. I've just realised that I haven't — haven't given you a proper cuddle yet Nanty — (*goes over, puts his arms around her*) there, now I feel safe, eh Daddy? From temptation and harm.

DAISY. Aaaah — aaaah — I always say you're the feeling one, don't I Jasper, feel things so quickly — anyway that's cheered you up, has it, I knew it would, didn't I Jasper, and it's a malt, you know — I asked for a malt — and now you can relax and tell us some of your funny stories about your life at the B.B.C. — I was just thinking the other day about my favourite, wasn't I, Jasper, that Hugh Rhys-what's-it on the religious talks programme of yours, the one who does the interviewing sometimes you used to keep us in stitches about, every time I hear him talking things over with Bishops and atheists and such I laugh out loud, I do, don't I Jasper, he sounds so solemn and Welsh but there he was getting himself locked in his office cupboard with his secretary and she thought — oh dear, all those scratches, poor man! (*Laughing.*) — And that quarrel with his wife over the dish-washer he insisted took saucepans and suds all over the kitchen floor short-whatnotting the fridge and the ice-cream gateau for his daughter's birthday melting into the fish for the cat — oh dear, oh dear — (*laughing*) what's he been up to recently, your Hugh-Rhys-what's-it, something hilarious, do tell us?

BENEDICT (*who has moved away from* DAISY, *grinning fixedly, his hands locked behind his back*). He's — um — actually he's dead, Nanty.

DAISY. What dear?

BENEDICT. Dead.

DAISY. Good Heavens do you hear that, Jasper, Hugh Rhys-thing — but how, how dear?

BENEDICT. Oh it was a — well as a — what happened apparently — (*Stops.*)

DAISY. What dear?

BENEDICT (*looks yearningly towards the scotch*). Well — well actually Nanty do you mind — (*Goes and sits down some distance from the scotch.*) if we — I — I don't go into it at the moment I'm — you see it — it upsets me to think about because in a way, well, in as much as I used to — to make him a bit of a butt and forgot how fond — how fond — you know what I mean, don't you Daddy, perhaps you could explain — explain to Nanty? (*Sits head lowered.*)

There is a slight pause. Off, the sound of boys' voices, and HENRY's *getting louder as they advance in a rush.*

HENRY (*off*). No, no Piers don't — don't shoot —

DAISY. What, what are they doing — right up — after all I've told —

A ball bounces into the room and towards JASPER. DAISY *runs after it, catches it.*

Of all the — of all the —

HENRY (*bounds in through the french windows breathing hard and sweating*). Oh golly — everyone all right?

DAISY. Well dear, it nearly bounced into your father's face, didn't it, Jasper?

HENRY. Oh, sorry Daddy — (*takes the ball from* DAISY) all right boys (*going to the french windows*) now keep it down at the bottom — right to the bottom — (*Throws the ball out.*)

DAISY. Yes dear, but you see I can't help worrying about the windows —

HENRY. No, further down, Tom — right down — (*turns*) we're going to the Piece soon Nanty, so don't worry —

DAISY. I know dear, so couldn't they wait until then — because even at the bottom there are the outhouse windows —

HENRY (*has gone to the drinks table, squirted himself some soda water*). Whew! (*Draining it off.*) You were wise to stay out of that, Ben, I remind me of that chap, I told you about him, didn't I Daddy — (*Squirts some more.*)

DAISY. You do see what I mean, don't you dear?

HENRY. — did a dozen laps around the park in the sun, gulped down a jug of lemonade, dropped dead.

DAISY. I don't want to spoil their fun, you know that dear, but — what, Good Heavens, why?

HENRY. Bad heart, Nanty.

DAISY. Well then why did he do it, run a dozen times around in the heat, any fool knows that's madness, don't they Jasper, why did he dear?

HENRY. Well, actually, now I come to think of it, because I told him to, Nanty.

DAISY. What, oh well of course that's different dear — but why did you?

HENRY. I must have thought he needed the exercise, I suppose. Perhaps if he'd taken enough of it earlier, he wouldn't have killed himself taking it later.

DAISY. So really he only had himself to blame, you mean, dear.

HENRY. Well, no. Really he had me to blame, didn't he? Or would have, if he'd survived. But to be fair to myself I didn't tell him to do his running in the midday sun, nor to gulp down ice-cold lemonade afterwards. At least I hope I didn't. But on the other hand I certainly didn't warn him not to, either. But then I didn't know at the time he had a bad heart. And nor did he, come to that. Still, we got to the right diagnosis between us at the end, didn't we? Poor chap. I liked him rather a lot, he played the clarinet for the L.S.O., I always try not to think of him every time I hear that Mozart piece you're so fond of Daddy, how does it go — you remember it Ben? (*Tries to hum a few bars.*)

DAISY. Oh, I know — (*Hums it very pleasantly.*)

HENRY *joins in.* DAISY *and* HENRY *hum the opening section.*

HENRY (*squirts more soda water*). And here I am myself, my stomach packed with casserole, golly it was good Nanty, wasn't it Ben, *and* jacket potatoes and those doughy things —

DAISY. Dumplings, dear, did you like them?

HENRY. Oh damn!

DAISY. What dear?

HENRY. I'm on call today and I think I forgot to leave your

number Daddy — well, I expect they'll know where I am. And anyway the call I don't make may save a life, eh? (*Laughs.*)

DAISY. Oh don't be silly Henry, you're a very good doctor, isn't he Jasper, isn't he Ben, a very good doctor, Henry —

MARIANNE (*enters from left flourishing a child's pottie*). Dum-dee-dee-dum-dum-dee-dee-dum — it was under my seat all the time, Nanty. In the van.

DAISY. What, oh good dear, I'm so glad — but isn't he a very good doctor, Henry?

MARIANNE. I should jolly well say he is, who says he isn't?

DAISY. Henry, dear.

MARIANNE. Oh ho, at it again, are we, hubby mine, I don't know what's been getting into him recently apart from the usual overwork, but the only thing wrong with him is that he's too jolly good a doctor, isn't he Gramps, and cares far too much and won't let himself let up for a minute, have you heard about his latest acquisition, I bet he hasn't even mentioned her, has he?

DAISY. Who, dear?

MARIANNE. Mrs O'Killiam, Nanty.

DAISY. Oh, is that the lady whose hair has been falling out, and wants a golden wig on the National Heath —

MARIANNE. No no Nanty, that's poor old ga-ga Mrs MacDougall, Henry's wangled her into a home at last, Gramps, although it was virtually over her dead body, wasn't it darling, no Mrs O'Killiam's a real case, in fact she's simply the most desperate case in the whole practice, Gramps, none of the others will touch her with a barge-pole.

HENRY. Now darling, that isn't quite true —

MARIANNE. Oh yes it is, darling, you know perfectly well that our Ancient Wedderspoon and our young Casanova Billy Hodges made absolutely certain that decent old Henry Muggins here would be the one to get landed with her, her husband's in jail for some quite unspeakable offence against an eighty year old woman, Gramps —

DAISY. Why, what did he do to her?

MARIANNE. Well, for one thing he —

HENRY. Darling, I don't think — um you know —

MARIANNE. All right darling, for Nanty's sake —

DAISY. No no, I like hearing about things like that, don't I Jasper?

MARIANNE. Anyway Gramps, as if that wasn't bad enough she's got two brutes of sons about twelve and fourteen who are always in trouble with the police themselves —

HENRY. Well, of course with their background —

MARIANNE. Oh I know darling, absolutely *no* chance, and a little girl called Carla —

HENRY. Wanda, darling.

MARIANNE. Who's hydrocephalic, Gramps.

DAISY. What, dear?

MARIANNE. Water on the brain, Nanty. (*Holding her hands away from her head.*)

DAISY. Oh, we've got one of those, haven't we Jasper, he rides past here on his bicycle looking like Humpty Dumpty poor thing —

MARIANNE. But the worst of it is she's in a dreadful way herself, Nanty, I shall never forget Henry's description of her the first time he saw her, Gramps, he said he said to himself as soon as he clapped eyes on her, 'Hello! Carcinoma!' didn't you darling?

DAISY. Hello who, dear?

HENRY. Although actually I was wrong, it's almost certainly a form of anorexia nervosa —

DAISY. What, dear?

MARIANNE. Good old fashioned despair, Nanty, that's what it jolly well is, Gramps, isn't it darling? And because old Henry Muggins here's bothered to show a little interest and listen to her problems — well, she's called him around every night this week, and after surgery too, he comes back looking grey with fatigue, Nanty, and the only time I've heard him utter a word of complaint is about the smell —

DAISY. Why, isn't it nice?

MARIANNE. Absolutely indescribable from what Henry says,
isn't it darling, — and this morning, Gramps, just as we were
leaving one of her boys turned up and told Henry his mum
wanted him straight away —

HENRY. But I really don't mind darling —

MARIANNE. Oh, I saw that look on your face before of course
he said of course, Gramps, and you would have gone too,
wouldn't you, if I hadn't asked him if it couldn't wait until
this evening, and do you know what he said, you didn't hear,
did you darling, the little squat one with the dribble and the
funny lip, he said — well, he'd fucking well better come then.

DAISY. What dear?

MARIANNE. Sorry everybody, but that's what he said.

HENRY. Oh, it's his normal vocabulary, he talks to everybody
like that, and I *am* on call darling.

MARIANNE. Yes darling, when aren't you on call? But you try
asking young Casanova B. or the Ancient W. to give up their
Saturday evenings for the Mrs O'Killiams of the world and
you'd get a pretty dusty answer, Gramps, I can tell you — and
now I've sorted you out, hubby mine, I'd better get this to
Nindy before it's too late if it isn't already, I glimpsed her from
the window a moment ago looking suspiciously thoughtful —

DAISY. Oh and thank you for doing the dishes, dear!

MARIANNE. What, oh golly, Nanty, did you mean for me to do
them?

DAISY. What, you mean you haven't you mean!

MARIANNE. No Nanty, I'm sorry, I haven't.

DAISY. But I saw you at the sink, you see, so I assumed — I wish
I'd known you weren't going to do them dear, because then I
could have got them over and done with by now myself, you see.

MARIANNE. Well honestly Nanty, one moment we were all in
the kitchen, and then Jenny'd gone —

DAISY. To get the muffins, dear.

MARIANNE. And then old Margaret had sloped off somewhere —
and then you'd vanished —

DAISY. Only because I was worred about the ball and the
windows —

MARIANNE. So it didn't cross my mind — and then I thought
I'd better have one more look for this because I know how
you hate it when — oh golly, well let me deal with Nindy and
I'll come back and do your dishes for you, all right? (*Goes out
through the french windows.*)

DAISY. No no dear I'll do them, I don't mind doing them, oh I do
hope she didn't think I meant, Henry you don't think she
thought I meant —

HENRY. No no Nanty, of course she didn't — but hey, I haven't
asked after your headaches — Nanty's been getting some very
bad headaches, Ben, hasn't she Daddy — (*Putting his arm
around* DAISY.)

DAISY. Oh they've been terrible recently, haven't they Jasper?
I've tried doing what you said, lying on a hard surface in a dark
room with moist pads over my eyes, but it doesn't stop the
throbbing or the nose-bleeds, does it Jasper?

HENRY. Nose-bleeds?

DAISY. Oh yes, terrible nose-bleeds and a humming in my ears
and seeing things double —

HENRY. I see. Well, Nanty, I think we ought to have someone
take a proper look at you, I can't promise he'll cure them but I
won't let him make them any worse.

DAISY. Oh Henry — aaaah — so kind, so thoughtful — oh and look
dear, tell Marianne she's not to touch the dishes, I never meant
her to, you know — they won't take me a minute tell her —
(*Going out through the arch.*)

HENRY. Actually Daddy, I think I'd better try and fix up an
appointment for Nanty as soon as possible — nothing to worry
about, just a few tests, X-rays, that sort of thing — all quite
routine, but to put our minds at rest, we don't want anything
happening to our Nanty, do we, Ben?

BENEDICT (*who has been gazing at floor, hands locked*). Mmmm?

HENRY. You all right?

BENEDICT. Oh. Oh well um — yes, yes. Thanks.

HENRY. I must say it's terrific to have you here again after all this time.

BENEDICT. Oh. Yes. Thanks. Thanks Henry.

HENRY. And Maggie too.

BENEDICT. Oh she was very keen to come. Very keen. Very very keen.

HENRY. Oh. Well that's flattering, eh Daddy? Where is she, by the way, I've hardly had a chance to speak to her.

BENEDICT. No.

HENRY. What?

BENEDICT. What?

HENRY. Maggie?

BENEDICT. Oh. Oh yes.

HENRY. Has she gone out?

BENEDICT. Yes. Yes I think so, yes. For a walk, hasn't she Daddy — something to do with her novel you see. She gets these fits. Inspiration, I suppose. Yes.

HENRY. Are you sure you're all right, Ben?

BENEDICT. No. No I seem — something slightly wrong with my — my stomach — perhaps those doughnuts in the casserole — but very queasy.

HENRY. I'll get you some Alka Seltzer, where is it Daddy?

BENEDICT. What — oh no, no, not Alka Seltzer, never works for me besides I don't want to make a fuss — I'll tell you — I'll tell you what, (*getting up*) perhaps a drop — just a little drop of this might do something for me (*picks up the glass with a trembling hand, takes an enormous gulp*) have to be careful though, eh Daddy, no back-sliding, eh, you see, Henry, I was telling Daddy, I've given this stuff up virtually at last, haven't I, Daddy? I go to a chap, you see.

HENRY. A chap?

BENEDICT. Yes. His name's Vintross. A bit of a genius in my view. He's been treating me for — things.

HENRY. Oh. A psychiatrist.

BENEDICT. No. A pediatrician, actually. But he does things like me on the side. Privately. God you should see his eyes when he's doing hypnosis, I was telling Daddy about them, wasn't I, Daddy? (*Pouring himself more scotch.*) They're the deepest brown eyes I've ever seen, and they burn, burn, down — he's bloody expensive, you can imagine.

HENRY. Yes. Yes. I can.

BENEDICT. But then that's part of his treatment, you see. Charges the equivalent of a double scotch for every three minutes of his time, he worked it out at. You're not cured, he said, until you get my bill. If you can look at it without taking a drink, there's hope, and if you pay it you won't be able to afford a drink, apart from meths, of course, and if you don't pay it, I sue. (*Laughs.*) Vintage Vintross, that is. Jokes are a part of his style.

HENRY. Oh — oh well he sounds just the job, doesn't he Daddy?

MATTHEW *enters through french windows, stands uncertainly.*

Oh hello Mat, and what have you been up to?

MATTHEW. Oh — um — well um — nothing um — (*Laughs.*)

HENRY. How's the soccer coming?

MATTHEW. Oh — well I mean um — you know.

HENRY. Made a team yet?

MATTHEW. Well — just the house team.

HENRY. Oh, well that's jolly good — isn't it Ben — congratters, Mat.

MATTHEW. Oh — well, um, thanks. (*Laughs.*)

HENRY. Oh and hey, I don't know if Marianne mentioned to you — we're taking the boys to the Piece soon for a footer around — why don't you come along and show them what you can do, and then show me how to do it, eh?

MATTHEW. Oh — well um — I — um — Mummy — Mummy asked me to go for a walk with her, you see — I — I — was meant to meet her at the baker's but um well you haven't seen her um?

HENRY. She hasn't been through here.

MATTHEW. Oh well she's probably gone looking — I'd better — better go and see if — um — (*Makes towards the exit, left.*)

HENRY. Anyway we'll be on the Piece later if you *do* want a game —

MATTHEW. Um — right — right — (*He goes out.*)

BENEDICT (*who has poured himself more scotch*). God he's getting like Dick isn't he — it makes the brain to reel and the heart to lurch how like Dick he's getting, doesn't it, is he top-dog at school, the way Dick used to be?

HENRY. Well actually that reminds me — I was going to mention it Daddy — and I'm glad you're here Ben, you can tell me what you think — you see I had a letter from his housemaster the other day, he seems to think of me as in sort of loco parentis and he didn't want to worry Jenny with it — but he's a little concerned about our Mat. Says he's been rather withdrawn this term — well, since Dick's death — well, I suppose that's hardly surprising, but apparently although he's dropped every one of his old chums he's taken up with a boy — well, quite a bit younger than himself and — in a nutshell, the housemaster isn't too keen on it. Thinks it's all a bit too hot-housey. That's why he's wangled Mat into the football team, to make him mix more you see, although actually Mat's not too good at football, but then this friend of his doesn't play at all. He's an asthmatic.

BENEDICT. Ah-hah! One of those, eh?

HENRY. What? Well, you see what troubles me is I'm not sure he should interfere at all — I mean, the football's all right, *if* Mat comes to enjoy it — but otherwise well this relationship may be filling an important need, mayn't it, and then given how delicate — delicate these matters are, especially at that age — well, what do you think, Daddy?

BENEDICT (*laughs*). God, doesn't it bring it back though?

HENRY. What?

BENEDICT. All of it — the sodomy, buggery, public-school duggery — much more fun than State schools, give them ten quid a week, kit them up with contraceptives, hand them a list of V.D. clinics, pack pot into their lunch-boxes, nothing furtive, nothing passionate, nothing to prepare them for life —

hey, remember old Prothero, Hen, old Prothero, did we ever tell you about old Prothero, Daddy, used to come and sit on the edge of the bed after lights, tucking in the middle-school chappies, and if there'd been a caning he'd want to inspect the stripes, put on ointment —

HENRY. Golly yes, old Cheeks! (*Laughs.*)

BENEDICT. That's it! Cheeks — Cheeks Prothero! Had a crush on Dick, didn't he Hen — and old Coote — Coote Wilson — and — all of them come to think of it, didn't they Hen? Had crushes on Dick, fighting over him they were! Like bloody monkeys! God, I'm glad you sent us to one of the best schools in the country, Daddy, aren't you Hen?

HENRY. I certainly don't think it did us any harm.

BENEDICT (*pouring himself another drink*). Vintross is queer. Gay, I mean. Did I tell you?

HENRY. Is he? No, you didn't.

BENEDICT. He's got this Philippino house-boy. Opens the door, takes your coat. Got a pretty beaten look to him, so I expect there's a cupboard full of things, eh, handcuffs, leg-irons, whips, masks, S.S. uniforms — that sort of gay, you see. Ballsy-gay. Sometimes his eyes go just like a cat's — a vicious green. You know?

HENRY. The house-boy's?

BENEDICT. Vintross's. Vintross's eyes.

HENRY. I thought you said they were brown —

BENEDICT. No, no. Green, eh Daddy? Vicious green. Like a cat's.

HENRY. How's the stomach?

BENEDICT. Flat as a board. Keeps himself in top nick, you see. Probably with the Philippino, eh? (*Laughs.*)

HENRY. No, I meant yours. Is it settling down?

BENEDICT. Oh. Well still a bit — hey Hen I must show Hen, eh Daddy — Vintross's party posture — look — hands so — feet thus — (*tries to adopt it, still holding his glass, stumbles backwards*). Oooooooops!

HENRY *catches him.*

Thanks. See what I mean, bloody difficult.

HENRY. Yes. (*Watches him, looks anxiously towards* JASPER.) Oh — that reminds me — that little Welsh friend of yours, the one that got his finger stuck in his flies at the Israeli Embassy — we were having a good laugh about him just the other week, weren't we Daddy? What's he been — ? (*Laughing.*)

BENEDICT (*laughing*). Old Hugh Rhys — um —

HENRY. Yes —

BENEDICT (*stops laughing*). Oh. Dead, Henry.

HENRY. What?

BENEDICT. Dead. Yes. Dead.

HENRY. That little Welsh — good God, good God, but — but well how, Ben, what happened?

BENEDICT. Killed himself. Didn't he Daddy? Telling Daddy and Nanty earlier —

HENRY. But why?

BENEDICT. Don't know Henry. Don't know. All I know is that one night last week he got out of bed, told his wife he wanted some air, walked up to Hampstead Heath, took off his trousers, hanged himself.

HENRY. With his own trousers?

BENEDICT. They found a washing-line too, but it had got tangled in the tree.

HENRY. And he didn't leave a note — nothing to explain —

BENEDICT. Oh yes. He left a note. Pages and pages in fact. Must have spent the day writing it — alone in his office — pages and pages — pinned them to his shirt.

HENRY. Well, what did it say?

BENEDICT. Don't know. It rained during the night. Illegible. Every word. Pathetic, eh Daddy? Poor little Hugh Rhys — um —

There is a pause. HENRY *releases a sudden wild laugh.*

BENEDICT. What?

HENRY. Oh I'm sorry — so sorry — don't know where that came

from — I certainly didn't mean any disrespect to Hugh — Hugh Rhys um —

BENEDICT. That's all right, Hen, we know why you laughed, don't we Daddy, matter of fact I laughed myself when I heard — I mean trousers, tangled washing-line, unreadable suicide note — like all the other stories I used to tell about him. Right?

HENRY. Well yes, I suppose —

BENEDICT. Except this time he's dead, of course. That's the difference. But a big one. Crucial, in fact.

HENRY. Yes. Yes indeed.

BENEDICT. Isn't that right, Daddy? (*Pours himself more scotch.*) And of course appropriate. Hugh Rhys — um's death. An appropriate death. Like Dick's, in a sense. Eh? (*There is a pause.*) I mean, you think of Dick, the brightest and the best of us, eh, we know that, Daddy, don't we Henry, well of course he was, because he was just like you, Daddy, wasn't he, fellowships just like you, lectureships just like you, a readership just like you, would have ended up with a professorship just like you, maybe even an O.B.E., Daddy, just like you, and then a wife he loved, just like you, Daddy, I mean you loved Mummy didn't you, the tragedy of your life her death, wasn't it, if you see, and a son he adored, just as you adored him, and is turning out just like him as he went on turning out just like you. Apart from being dead. Just like Mummy. See Daddy.

HENRY. No. No. I don't think we do see, quite, Ben. But perhaps we shouldn't discuss —

BENEDICT. No no, look at it this way. Where was Dick different from Daddy? Where? A bit raffish, right? Bit of an adventurer, right? We all know his reputation with women, I mean even after he married Jenny, but that didn't stop him, did it, from bits and pieces we used to hear, at it all the time, wasn't he? (*Laughs.*) Reckless. Reckless and raffish — not like Daddy, oh, nobody's ever called you reckless and raffish, have they, Daddy? And so his motor-bike. See. See where that fits in. We all told him, we all warned him, after his accidents, his broken leg, his neck in plaster, but he went on, didn't he, roaring about on his motor-bike. And Daddy's never roared about on a motor-bike. Have you, Daddy? At least not to our knowledge. Eh Hen? See. See how it fits?

HENRY. Well Ben, not really and I — I — well um — (*Looks towards* JASPER.)

BENEDICT. Two sides of his nature, you see. The opposite. Roars over here, has one of his intimate chats with Daddy, and then later, far too late, when he was tired, his head spinning with Daddy's ideas and jokes and anecdotes and gossip, eh Daddy? What does he do? Does he stay the night? Upstairs in bed in his old room? Does he stay the night? No. Not old Dick. Back, back on his motor-bike, roaring off again — past Newmarket, past Baldock, Royston, Hitchin — faster and faster, and then off — off the road — hurtling right off the road and over the bank and into the tree into the dark! And we say — *we* say — if it hadn't been for his motor-bike Dick'd still be alive. True. But — but if it hadn't been for Daddy, then he wouldn't be dead. Vintross says. (*Pours himself more scotch.*) Now do you see?

HENRY. Well — um, Ben — look, what would Vintross say if he could see the amount of scotch you're knocking back, old chap?

BENEDICT. Say it was quite all right. As long as I can cope with it in a situation I can't cope with without it. That's what he'd say.

JENNY (*enters left*). Oh sorry — but has he come back, Matthew?

HENRY. Yes. But he went out again — I think he was looking for you —

BENEDICT. Hey Jen, we were just saying about Matthew — so like Dick, isn't he? So like him?

JENNY. Yes — yes I suppose he is —

BENEDICT. Henry was telling us about that letter he got from his housemaster — on his little sexual problems — don't you pay any attention, Jen, Dick had the same, used to steal too, didn't he, Hen, has Matthew started stealing yet? Well, don't worry, if he turns out like Dick he'll be all right, eh? Apart from being dead, I mean.

JENNY. Matthew's housemaster wrote to you?

BENEDICT. Saying Vintross says — Vintross —

DAISY. Who dear? Oh, that little Welsh friend of yours, so sad, so sad —

BENEDICT. When I was little, Nanty, made me eat and eat and eat —

DAISY. What, oh well dear, I did my best to keep your tummy full, of course I did, didn't I Jasper, but then you were such a greedy mite, you know, wasn't he Jasper, like Oliver Twist dear, always asked for more. (*Laughs.*)

BENEDICT. What?

DAISY. What dear?

There is a pause.

DAISY. Dear?

BENEDICT. Wanted to be our Mummy, didn't you Nanty? Take the place of my Mummy?

DAISY. What — oh oh no dear — oh no — I knew I could never take *her* place, didn't I Jasper, even though people said we were almost look-alikes, not usual you know in second cousins once removed except she had golden hair that came right down her back to sit on, sit on her own hair, she could, couldn't she Jasper, oh really very glamorous your mother dear, aaaah, such a pity she didn't live to see what you've become! —

BENEDICT. What?

DAISY. — Isn't it Jasper, she adored you all, didn't she Jasper?

BENEDICT. Me? Adored me? Me too?

DAISY. Well dear, it was different with you, you were just an insignificant scrap at the time, and always crying for a feed, you know, while Henry was bigger and she could talk to him and Dick — well Dick, she idolised, Dick — but then we all did, didn't we Jasper? Because he was so pretty and clever.

BENEDICT *laughs.*

What dear?

BENEDICT. Dead, Nanty. Gone. Pretty Dick. Clever Dick. Through the door in the wall. On his motor-bike.

DAISY. Yes, dear, I know dear. So sad.

BENEDICT. Why didn't you stop him?

DAISY. What dear?

BENEDICT. Why didn't you stop him, Nanty. Killing himself.
Why — why — ? Eh? Answer me that, Nanty!

DAISY. Oh really Benedict, oh really dear, I've told you before,
haven't I Jasper, every time you come down dear I've told you
this, you can't have forgotten, can he Jasper, I've told you and
told you dear I told him not to, didn't I Jasper, and if he'd
listened to me it wouldn't have happened, would it Jasper,
it's late I said, you're tired I said, stay the night, make him
stay the night, Jasper, didn't I Jasper, and he said, what was it
he said, or was it you Jasper, one of you said, oh nobody can
stay the night Daisy or Nanty whichever of you it was said it,
and they both laughed, the pair of them, and off he roared, off
he roared, poor silly boy, in that helmet pulled down and
those great gauntlets, and his head so low over the handle-bars,
roaring off, and I knew, I knew, if he'd listened to me it
wouldn't have happened, would it Jasper, but then nobody
listens to me, it was just the same with your mother you know,
when I told her to go straight to the doctor with that lump, I
knew that lump as soon as I saw it, didn't I Jasper, Rose, I said,
Rose, Rose —

BENEDICT *stumbles towards the door, left.*

What, where are you going, dear?

BENEDICT (*in a child's voice*). Old room, Nanty, lie down in my
old room when I was little Nanty —

DAISY. There's a good boy, aaaah, but oh, not your old room
dear, Matthew's in there, and all his things and Jenny's using
Dick's of course, they're staying the night you see, so you use
Henry's dear — Henry's old room —

BENEDICT *goes out.*

(*As she speaks the stage begins to darken.*) Did he hear, oh I
hope he heard, he always makes such a mess when he comes
down, not that it isn't lovely to see him, for your sake. I know
dear, but sometimes I think he tipples (*lifts her hand to her
mouth in a drinking movement*) a little too much, it's all very
well to say he needs relaxing but not when he turns things

upside down, and he takes after Rose that way, she liked her
glass too, but of course she didn't let it go to her head like
that, and oh why did he have to upset me with remembering
Rose and Dick poor dears, and now my head, pounding because
of the honking, pounding you know — and all the times I've
asked them not to let Tom — but then it's true, true nobody
listens to me, they go in and out and don't do the dishes and
make fusses but not one of them says about tea, what am I
meant to do about tea, Jasper, do I lay for everybody on the
assumption or what, do I, do I lay on the assumption, that's
what I want to know Jasper, well, that's what comes of letting
them treat me as the housekeeper, that's what they think I am,
well it won't do, it's not good enough, it's time they were told
what I really am, and you should tell them dear, yes, it's up to
you to tell them, Jasper, now we've got them all together and
— oh, good Heavens, oh no (*seeing the pot*) what's this doing —
but it's half full, you see, you see what I mean — left for me to
— sometimes I think Marianne — no wonder my head — my
poor head — (*begins to go out under the arch*) and oh, the
windows, I'm shutting the windows so they can't come in this
way (*shuts them*) and tramping mud (*locks them*) there, there,
at least I won't have mud this time — (*Going out through arch.*)

The stage continues to darken to half-light.

JASPER *lets out a sudden, terrible groan. Puts his head back.*

Curtain.

Act Two

The same. About an hour later. JASPER *as before. The stage is in semi-darkness. It is raining heavily. There is a sudden rattling at the windows.* MARIANNE's *voice,* HENRY's *urgently, with the cries of children.*

MARIANNE (*off*). Gramps — Gramps — are you there!

HENRY (*off*). Daddy — Daddy — can you hear me!

DAISY (*enters on the run through the arch*). No no, not there — not that way — oh it's so dark — (*turns on the lights*) I've opened the back-kitchen door — I've put a mat down in the back-kitchen — the back-kitchen dears please —

HENRY. For Heaven's sakes Nanty, we're getting — all right, but you go in that way, darling, I'm not having you get any wetter — Nanty — Nanty — open the door for Marianne!

DAISY. What, oh — (*opens the french windows*) oh, there you are dear, are you all right? I didn't mean you of course, just the children — I wanted to make sure they'd go around by the back-kitchen where I've put another mat especially you see —

MARIANNE (*during this enters, with a man's raincoat over her head, in Wellington boots*). I must say Nanty, I didn't expect you'd actually lock the door on us — but golly, what a business — (*Taking off her raincoat.*)

DAISY. Here dear — let me — (*Taking the coat.*)

MARIANNE. One minutes thumping the ball about, the next absolute buckets, like the Old Testament, Gramps — (*Lifts a leg.*) I say Nanty, do you mind —

DAISY. What, oh. (*Pulls at the boot.*) And the one in the back-kitchen had gone, I think the boys must have — (*Pulls the boot off.*)

MARIANNE (*staggering back*). Whhoops!

DAISY. All right dear? You know for football posts, I know they do sometimes.

MARIANNE *lifts the other leg.*

DAISY (*pulls it off*). So I had to put the one from the front door down — there, there we are —

MARIANNE. Thank goodness we had our bad weather gear in the van — we had to sprint like billy-oh to get it and then we thought Nindy had dropped her pot —

DAISY. What, oh no dear, her pot was here, where you left it. Half full and more.

MARIANNE (*laughing*). Yes, Henry remembered after we'd sent poor old Nigel haring back for it with my plastic bonnet over his head —

HENRY (*enters under the arch, towelling his head*). Phew, what a soaking —

DAISY. I'll just go and put these — you saw the mat, did you, Henry?

HENRY. What, Nanty?

DAISY. The mat. I put down the mat.

HENRY. Oh.

DAISY. Well, they did use it, dear, didn't they, I had to get it round from the front, you know, because the one at the back — I think the boys must have taken it for their football —

MARIANNE. No, they didn't Nanty. They haven't touched it, not after all the business last time when they were using it as a sleigh and you were jolly sharp with them.

DAISY. Oh, well as long as they've used the one I've just put down, they did didn't they, Henry?

HENRY. Well, actually Nanty, there wasn't a mat there.

DAISY. What, what do you mean, I've only just put it there, haven't I, Jasper? It can't have gone too.

HENRY. Well, Nanty, I can assure you, there's no mat there.

DAISY. Where?

HENRY. The kitchen.

DAISY. The kitchen! But I told you to go by the back-kitchen —
I opened the back-kitchen door especially — I told you —

HENRY. Oh sorry, I just heard kitchen —

DAISY. Oh good Heavens — and after all the trouble I went to
— well where are they now, what are they doing, and there'll
be mud on their boots — where are they?

HENRY. Now now, Nanty, don't panic, I've told them to take off
their shoes and dry and wash themselves and to sit quietly down
at the table.

DAISY. The table, which table?

HENRY. Well, the kitchen table.

DAISY. Why?

HENRY. Well, for their tea.

DAISY. Their tea! But they can't have digested their lunches yet!

MARIANNE. Well, you know the boys, they can be digesting their
lunches while they're eating their tea — (*Laughs.*)

DAISY. But I've laid for everybody, haven't I Jasper, I've laid for
everybody, a proper family tea — muffins and — rock-cakes
even —

MARIANNE. Oh, they don't need muffins and rock-cakes, just
some bread and butter and marmite and milk —

HENRY. We'll do it, Nanty, no need for you to bother yourself.

DAISY. Oh, it's not bothering myself I mind, I'm used to that,
aren't I, Jasper, the point is I laid tea for everybody, as nobody
told me any differently, can't they wait?

HENRY. They can't really, Nanty, no. I know it's unreasonable
of them, to be at the age when they're permanently hungry —

MARIANNE. And anyway Nanty, as you won't allow them
anywhere *but* the kitchen — and what can they do there *but*
eat — at least that's the way they see it —

DAISY. I've never said they can't go into the spare rooms
upstairs, I've never said that, although now you mention it

they couldn't because of course Jenny's in Dick's and now
Matthew wants one to himself he's in Benedict's and Benedict's
lying down in Henry's and they'd wake him, wouldn't they
Jasper?

MARIANNE. Well, of course, if Benedict needs to lie down —
Anyway, they've got to have it now because poor old Henry's
got to go and see Mrs O'Killiam —

DAISY. Who?

MARIANNE. — and it's all getting a bit — so, for goodness' sake
darling, let's give them their tea at home —

DAISY. What, take them home, you can't take them home, I've
sliced three loaves and buttered the slices, no no, you can't take
them home you know, not without their tea, can they Jasper?

HENRY. But Nanty, if it's asking too much of you —

DAISY. If they need their tea now, let them have it now, by all
means, I'll go and see to it straight away — here, Henry, you'd
better give me that — (*takes the towel away from him*) and I'll
put these in the back-kitchen — (*as she goes*) and oh, by the
way, if Nindy wants her pot you'll find it sluiced in the down-
lavatory.

There is a pause.

MARIANNE. Golly, well we seem to have put our foot in it again,
don't we darling, I don't know what it is about Nindy's pottie
that brings out the worst in Nanty, do you Gramps, all that fuss
over the soup tureen last week and then hiding it in the kitchen
cupboard did I tell you about that darling, before lunch when
she thought I'd forgotten it again, not that I hadn't learnt my
lesson though what could be less offensive than a toddler's wee,
I mean I wasn't going to dish it out as soup or anything —

HENRY. I think she's got one of her headaches, darling, and a bit
tired with it. You know.

MARIANNE. Oh. Oh well, poor old Nanty — I'd better go and
keep the peace.

HENRY. No, I'll go darling, you relax and have a jaw with Daddy,
you haven't had a proper one yet.

MARIANNE. Well, you *are* marvellous at dealing with her, I'll
take over later, when you've got her back under your thumb.

HENRY. Righto, darling. (*Goes out through the arch.*)

MARIANNE. Poor old Nanty, I know Henry's quite worried about those headaches of hers and now nose-bleeds and double vision he says, oh nothing sinister he's sure but still, you know how these things go if they're not watched, Gramps, that's all, and now our Henry's got it in hand so not to worry — (*settles on the sofa*) aaah, aaaah, I must say that's jolly nice, isn't it, now you put your feet up too — (*addressing her belly*) golly, all that springing about (*little pause, lets out a laugh*) do you know Gramps, there was a time I'd have done anything not to be alone with you, have I ever told you that, you used to scare me out of my wits, I mean when I first turned up as the girl that had bagged your Henry I used to quiver with terror at the mere thought of you, I mean, you being famously clever and a Professor and an O.B.E. even and Henry saying you were the wisest man he'd ever met, and all those books you'd written about books I couldn't even read, Chaucer and that lot, so in those days I had to say it to God instead even though I longed to say it to you, and now I realise I still haven't got around to saying it, even though you're jolly well nearly actually human at last as far as I am concerned — and it's only this, although I expect Henry would set fire to himself from embarrassment if he could hear me, but I'm going to say it anyway, it's thank you, Gramps. And thank you God still, of course. So thank you God and thank you Gramps. For my Henry. There! I've said it. (*Laughs, then suddenly serious.*) And there's something else I want to say, Gramps, and Henry wouldn't like that either, he's always on tenterhooks that I'm going to put my big foot in it over Dick's death, and that's why I've kept off the subject for so long, but you know Gramps there are times when I think we English, well we middle-class English types, what there's left of us, well we're all too jolly reticent about the really important things, perhaps that's always been our trouble, that we go on suffering in silence so everybody thinks they can go on getting anything they like from us down to our last stitch probably and we still wouldn't let out as much as a whimper, oh I'm not saying we should claw and scratch for what we want, just like the rest of them, I couldn't believe that and be old Henry's wife, could I? And I'm not saying we should go the whole Mediterranean hog over things like grief, either Gramps, with

screamings and wailings and teeth-gnashings and shrouded in
black and all that rot, but we don't jolly well have to creep
about and about as if we were ashamed of the dead, do we? I
mean, why can't we sit around over our evening sherries that
everybody sneers at so much, or our cups of tea or anyway
something English and admit to each other straight out how much
we loved him and miss him and have a good natter about him,
eh, Gramps, Henry doesn't, you know, not even with me, and
yet — and yet — well golly! Henry's (*little pause*) — I know
people just think of Henry as the rock and the brick and the
pillar, as if it were natural to him, that he can't help being
good old Henry so what's so jolly special about that, eh, they
don't know, they haven't the least idea what — but *we* do,
don't we Gramps, just because he doesn't go to pieces and
drink and go around being desperate and loony and gibbering
and being sick at the funeral — oh I'm sorry, Gramps, I don't
mean to get at Ben, I know he has his problems and I'm jolly
glad he's found the time to look in on us at last — although
from what Henry was saying — oh nothing disloyal, just
something he let drop, he's been at it again, perhaps that hasn't
helped Nanty's head — no, all I mean Gramps is *we* know how
Henry feels, well, perhaps even you don't, Gramps, how
deeply he — I mean, that night when Dick — he'd just come in,
he'd been over to see one of his desperates, an old man who'd
lost his wife and his leg in an accident, through no fault of his
own, I think, someone like that, anyway, and I was in bed and
I heard him doing his last rounds, as we call it, in and out of
the bedrooms whispering his goodnights and giving his kisses,
and then the 'phone rang, and he answered it, I heard his voice
from the hall, so calm, and I prayed he wouldn't have to go
out, why can't they let him alone to come to bed with me
where I was waiting for him, and then he came up and told me
what had happened and said he had to go straight out to be
with you because Nanty would only make things worse, oh he
didn't mean anything against Nanty, Gramps, only that, well —
I didn't hear him come back but at dawn I had a feeling and I
went down to the kitchen and there he was, sitting in a — in a
sort of madness of misery — he had blood in his mouth and on
his chin where he'd struck himself — but his first thought was
of me, *he* was consoling *me*, and by the time the children came
down he'd washed himself and was cheerful for them, and

jolly, as he always is, and he took the boys to school, and then
on to be with you and then back to his surgery and then back
to you Gramps, being the rock and the brick and the temple —
but that night he stayed downstairs again, I heard him crying
out once or twice — because he doesn't wear his bruises all over,
all over like a squashy tomato and he makes jokes against
himself, people don't realize how easily bruised my Henry is,
but anybody who cares as much about other people are, aren't
they, Gramps? Even if they've gone through life thinking that
because they're the second son they're somehow second rate —
oh Gramps, I'm sorry, I don't mean you didn't give Henry his
fair does of love and attention when he was little so it must be
your fault and all that fashionable rot, and poor old Nanty did
her best too, and anyway if his missing out on anything's made
him what he is, then I'm jolly glad he missed out, because
otherwise I might have missed out on him and you don't have
to tell me how difficult it is to do right by them every second
of every minute of every day, I'm as bad as Nanty with my lot
sometimes, I know I am, why just the other afternoon I had
quite a funny moment, well it wasn't funny at the time, oh it
was the usual sort of thing, Gramps, Nigel and Simon were
quarrelling in the cubby-room over whose turn on the skate-
board I think it was while I was dishing up their six o'clocks,
horlicks for Nigel and Tom and Piers, ovaltine for Simon and
Nindy and me, and I was stirring away as usual, out of the
corner of my eye I caught myself watching them at it, Simon
had the skate-board hugged to his chest and Nigel trying to
struggle it out of his arms, and on their faces there were such
expressions, but oh, perfectly normal, Gramps, golly! (*Laughs.*)
They were just being children, humans, that's all, but still I
caught myself, I was the horrible one, caught myself wishing
they were, all of them, Tom and Piers and Nindy too, though
Piers and Tom were upstairs quite innocent in front of
childrens' television for all I knew and Nindy was sitting in her
highchair humming bubbles out quite nicely and for all I knew
feeling quite nice, but all of them, I wished all of them, this
one too, isn't it a horrible Mums? (*To her belly.*) Oh, it was just a
flash, Gramps, just an out of the corner of my eye thing, deep
and midnight stuff, but it had never happened before, you see
Gramps, so of course now I keep remembering it, it pops in and

out when I least expect it, that I actually wished — oh, I know
I'm not like that really, or the house would be full of corpses,
(*laughs*) all I mean is that it's a jolly funny business, life and
parenthood and all that — and if my Henry weren't around,
now that this thought's taken to popping in and out more and
more and sometimes all the time even — I might be in danger
of going — well, a bit potty. (*Laughs.*) What do you think,
Gramps?

MARGARET *enters. She is smoking.*

MARIANNE. Oh hello Maggie!

MARGARET *smiles.*

But I say, you haven't been out in this have you?

MARGARET. Yes.

MARIANNE. Golly, why?

MARGARET. Oh — for a walk.

MARIANNE. Gosh, didn't you get wet?

MARGARET. I took shelter in a 'phone box.

MARIANNE. Oh. But it's still at it, isn't it? How did you get
back?

MARGARET. In a taxi.

MARIANNE. Gosh, that was lucky, how did you get hold of
one?

MARGARET. I telephoned for it.

MARIANNE. Oh, of course. Not lucky then, just jolly sensible
(*laughs*).

MARGARET. Do you know where Ben is?

MARIANNE. No — oh, yes — upstairs, didn't Nanty say Gramps,
having a snooze.

MARGARET. Oh (*makes to go off*).

MARIANNE. Why don't you let him get on with it, as he probably
needs it from what Henry says — I mean, it's such a long time
since we've seen each other and I'm longing to hear all about
your success, aren't we Gramps?

MARGARET *hesitates.*

Come on then!

MARGARET *sits down.*

Jolly good! Now — now then tell us all about your — whoops!
(*Little pause.*) Whoops! (*Little pause.*) And again! He still thinks
we're footering about on the Piece with Henry and the boys —
and a hefty kick he's developing too, aren't you? (*Looks down,
pats her stomach.*) I just realized the other day that that's why
I always assume my babies are he's, even Nindy, they've all had
such hefty kicks, even Nindy (*laughs*) although Tom was the
worst, I honestly think he decided to boot his way out, while
Nigel was a bit more like a clog-dancer Henry used to say
(*laughs*).

There is a pause.

MARGARET (*as if making an effort*). And which would you
prefer this time?

MARIANNE. What?

MARGARET. Boy or girl?

MARIANNE. Do you know, I really don't mind, Maggie. I mean, I
suppose a sister for Nindy would be convenient. At least for
Nindy. But then so would another brother for Nigel, Simon,
Tom and Piers. Or a sister for Nigel, Simon, Tom and Piers,
come to think of it. Or a brother for Nindy. Not that *they've*
given it a thought one way or another, and Henry says he'll
take what comes as usual, and Gramps hasn't expressed any
views either way, have you Gramps, so I'll settle for my
routine, run-of-the-mill eight pounder thank you very much
God, if you know what I mean (*laughs*).

MARGARET. I think so.

MARIANNE. What?

MARGARET. Well, you incline towards a baby, and you have a
strong preference for either sex.

MARIANNE. Yes. (*Little pause.*) I really shouldn't make such a
display, should I?

MARGARET. I don't see how you could help it.

MARIANNE (*laughs*). No, that's true enough. Anyway, enough of babies! I was saying to Henry on our way here this morning that the few times you and I have had a proper natter it's really only me nattering away about the one I'm in the process of having or the ones I've already had and you have to go through the same old motions and ask the same old boring questions, and this time I wasn't going to let you, especially with so much to talk about about yourself, I mean blossoming virtually overnight into a famous writer and tele-person even, golly, you must be jolly chuffed!

MARGARET. Well, um —

MARIANNE. No honestly, I'd be swollen with pride, wouldn't I Gramps! And what have the reviews been like, I've scarcely seen any.

MARGARET. Oh. What are called mixed.

MARIANNE. Jolly good, eh Gramps? One of the ones I read was very nice. It said you were like a scalpel, gosh (*laughs*) I think it was meant to be nice, anyway.

MARGARET. That was *The Times*.

MARIANNE. Was it, you read them all then, do you, I don't know how you could bear to. I mean the bad ones. If there were any.

MARGARET. I'd rather read them myself than have them read out to me by friends.

MARIANNE. You're absolutely right, anyway what does it matter what they say, it's been a great success, hasn't it, and I'll bet that infuriates them.

MARGARET. Who?

MARIANNE. The ones who were snide and snarky, there was one I came across made me absolutely livid!

MARGARET. Oh. *The Guardian*.

MARIANNE. No, it wasn't *The Guardian*. Could it have been *The Telegraph*?

MARGARET. No.

MARIANNE. Oh, that was a good one, then?

MARGARET. They didn't review it.

There is a pause.

MARIANNE. Anyway, as long as *you* think it's good, that's what counts, isn't it Gramps?

MARGARET. Thank you. (*Lights another cigarette.*) And have you read it yet?

MARIANNE. Oh gosh, yes, haven't I said?

MARGARET. I had the impression you called out something at lunch. As you passed the dumplings.

MARIANNE. I know, it's such a shambles, isn't it, I was just saying to Henry that our lot must do a marvellous job of putting you and Ben off family life (*laughs*).

There is a pause.

MARGARET. And what did you say?

MARIANNE. What?

MARGARET. As you passed the dumplings.

MARIANNE. Oh — oh golly, nothing profound, knowing me. Just the usual congratters, I expect.

There is a pause.

MARGARET. Did you enjoy it?

MARIANNE. Oh — oh, now I've got to be careful not to plonk my great foot in it, but to be honest I can't say I actually *enjoyed* it, Maggie, I didn't know you wanted me to, I mean let's face it, it isn't just a jolly good snorter of a read, like the usual stuff I get my nose into, for one thing you have to be on your toes all the time, but I admit I've done my share of boasting about our being fellow-sisters-in-law, especially after that T.V. thing.

MARGARET. I'm glad you got something out of it.

MARIANNE. Of course we always knew you were brainy, but not so devastatingly brainy, eh, Gramps? The way you conjured up all those weird people and being so — so ruthless and — and devastating about the whole bunch of them. Am I being very feeble.

MARGARET. You found them weird, did you?

MARIANNE. You and old Ben don't actually *know* types like that, do you?

MARGARET. Yes, actually.

MARIANNE. Then no wonder you put them in a book, that's where they belong, isn't it Gramps? Whoops — he's at it again! (*Laughs.*)

There is a pause.

But tell me, how long did it take you to write, I can never remember when you started, but you seem to have been at it for years.

MARGARET. Two.

MARIANNE. Years?

MARGARET. Yes.

MARIANNE. Golly!

MARGARET. From conception to delivery.

MARIANNE. Gosh! Whoops, now stop it!

MARGARET. I know. Especially when you think what can be turned out in nine months.

MARIANNE. What do you —, oh, I see! (*Laughs.*) Oh, but anyone can produce one of these, can't they — or is that what you meant?

MARGARET. No, I think I meant — (*Stops.*)

MARIANNE. What, Maggie?

MARGARET. Oh — merely that we're very different people.

MARIANNE. Who, you and I, you mean? Well, I'll say we are! (*Little pause.*) Although when you think about it we're only different because you're brainy and I'm not, otherwise we're at least women, after all, aren't we?

MARGARET. Which amounts to what? That we've both got wombs for breeding and breasts for feeding but we're under no obligation to use what brains we've got for thinking.

MARIANNE. Yes, I know, but isn't it awful how they rust over if we don't.

MARGARET. Which?

MARIANNE. What?

MARGARET. Which rust over, our wombs, our tits or our brains?

MARIANNE. Oh, I was thinking of myself, so I meant brains of course. But perhaps all three when you put it like that.

There is a pause.

MARGARET (*lights another cigarette, puffs at it, looks at* MARIANNE). Actually, my reproductive organs work with regulation efficiency.

MARIANNE. Oh. Oh, well jolly good, eh Gramps?

MARGARET. Otherwise I wouldn't have needed two abortions.

MARIANNE. Oh. Oh, I didn't know.

MARGARET. I know.

MARIANNE. I'm sorry.

MARGARET. What for?

MARIANNE. Well, if I've been clumsy.

MARGARET. I don't think you've been at all clumsy. I had the first when I was nineteen, to prevent an unwanted baby by an unwanted middle-aged school-teacher.

MARIANNE. I suppose somebody might have wanted him though, mightn't they?

MARGARET. His wife didn't, when he tried to go back to her.

MARIANNE. I meant the baby. Because of all the people desperate to adopt, you know.

MARGARET. Yes, I do know. But I wasn't prepared to be their beast of burden. The second was Benedict's, two years ago.

MARIANNE. You really don't have to tell us about it, does she Gramps?

MARGARET. Oh, I don't mind.

MARIANNE. But I do rather, I'm afraid.

MARGARET. Really, what of? You've always been so open and free about that aspect of your life. Not that the Ben abortion's particularly interesting, I admit. But it happened to coincide with my beginning my novel, and as I didn't want a baby anyway, I wasn't going to let it muck up my creative processes, if you follow. Fortunately there's a bright lady gynaecologist in Hampstead who also writes comic plays for the feminist fringe — her most celebrated is called 'The Miracle of Life and How to Stop it' — who was naturally sympathetic — actually she considers every sperm her personal enemy because they look like that little theatre critic on *The Sunday Times*, so killing them off is a pleasure as well as a duty, she says — (*Laughs.*)

MARIANNE. Aren't we sophisticated, eh, Gramps?

MARGARET *looks away as if she hasn't heard.*

MARIANNE. *I said*, aren't we sophisticated.

MARGARET. Oh, I'm sorry. I thought you were talking to Gramps —

MARIANNE *stands up, let's out a sudden cry.*

MARGARET. What?

MARIANNE. I can't — I won't (*rising, takes a few steps*). Oooh-oooh —

MARGARET. What, what is it? (*Going to her.*)

MARIANNE. Sofa — sofa — Henry — quickly — ooooh — (*Collapses awkwardly on it.*)

MARGARET. Oh my God, oh my God, I'll get him — (*Goes towards the arch.*)

MATTHEW *has appeared at the french windows. He stands uncertainly watching. He enters hesitant.*

MARIANNE (*holding MARGARET's arm*). No no — my leg — please rub it — quickly.

MARGARET *seizes her leg, begins to rub.*

MATTHEW. Um, if — if you see Mummy — um —

MARIANNE. No, no, the other one, the other one (*irritably*) quick — quick — rub!

MATTHEW. I'll be — um — I'll be up in my room —

Goes out left quickly.

MARIANNE. Oh God! Oh God! Rub - rub!

HENRY (*runs easily through the arch*). Ah, the old crampers, eh darling — here, let me, Maggie, I've got the trick of it — (*Takes MARIANNE's leg, begins to massage it expertly.*)

MARIANNE. Aaaah, aaah — (*with increasing relief*) that's it, aaah, clever old stick — there now — Golly, poor old Maggie, she thought I was going to litter right at her feet, didn't you Maggie?

HENRY (*laughs, turns, sees MARGARET's face*). Are you all right?

MARGARET. Yes thank you. As everything seems to be under control I think I'll go and look at my husband.

MARIANNE. Jolly good! (*And as MARGARET goes out.*) Not that I'd have dared, would I Gramps? Litter I mean, she'd probably have trampled on him, well, at least now we know, don't we Gramps, she's not infertile or frigid, darling, she has them killed, she sat there boasting about it, didn't she Gramps, she was horrible, quite horrible, wasn't she Gramps, so you come here for a minute, come on.

HENRY *hesitates, sits beside her.* MARIANNE *takes his arm, wraps it around her, leans into him.*

There, now I feel safe, no-one can harm us now, can they, we won't let her get you — aah — squeeze me, a little pressure, *you* know — that's right — aaah — aaah —

HENRY. Well, don't get too comfy darling, or you'll go into one of your snoozes.

MARIANNE. No, no, course I won't — course I won't — (*In a little girl's voice.*)

HENRY *strokes MARIANNE's hair, pushes a lock back, looks into her face. After a moment an expression of enormous sadness comes over his face. Then he looks at JASPER, smiles.*

DAISY *enters under the arch.*

DAISY. Oh, oh you're *both* in here now are you, no, no, it's all right, it's just that Henry suddenly vanished and there's a terrible squabble over those blasted rock-cakes, I said they could only have half each because Jenny got them specially for Matthew, didn't she Jasper, instead of muffins as I asked,

and now they're all at each other's throats because somebody
took Piers's half —

HENRY *makes to get up.*

MARIANNE. No, you don't, you've done your stint with Nanty
and you've still got Mrs O'Killiam to come —

DAISY *goes out under the arch.*

And oh — Gramps. Thank you God and Gramps.

HENRY. What for?

MARIANNE. Oh, just something Gramps gave me years ago,
hubby mine! (*Tweaks his cheek, goes out.*)

HENRY. What? Oh — oh I see — (*Lets out his sudden strange
laugh.*) Golly, sorry, sorry Daddy (*does it again*) must be —
must be what they mean by *fou rire* — old Marianne's thanking
— and — and Mrs O'Killiam — because you see, well —
remember that little lecture you gave us a few decades back,
but aimed particularly at Dick, of course, on *hubris*, and I
remember thinking it didn't matter that I didn't understand
what *hubris* was, because whatever it was, I'd never be up to it,
from the sound of it, if you see. But now I realize the essential
fact about it — *hubris* — that you don't have to be a king or a
Dick to be capable of it, it's quite democratic, at least these
days, I mean just thinking you can do a little, a very little, well,
good, is enough, isn't it Daddy? That's *hubris* too, thinking you
can do good? Or am I — perhaps I'm trying to make it all
sound more — more grand morally, more interesting and
philosophical than it really — because actually she's not really
quite as — as grotesque as somehow I'd led Marianne to
believe, I mean it's true that she's thin, she was certainly off
her food, from depression, really terrible depression, but her
face — her face is — rather touching, delicate and there's
something in her eyes, behind the fatigue and giving up —
rather — well, rather lovely, haunting — she touches one, you
see, in her despair. I don't know why I led Marianne to believe,
even right at the beginning that she was — of course it's true
her boys are brutes, that's certainly true and — and the little
girl, well she's not a hydrocephalic but she does have adenoids
that give her face a swollen — from time to time — and her

husband, well it's nothing to do with an eighty-year-old woman,
I don't know why I — I — you know how truthful I've always
been, perhaps it was simply lack of practice led me to — to —
(*laughs*) he's certainly been in trouble with the police, of
course, for something to do with cars, I think it was, and he's
abandoned her and as I say she is — quite naturally — given the
way life's treated her — the victim of appalling depressions —
and — and — but please don't believe I ever, I ever intended,
planned, or wanted to — actively wanted to — make love to
her. I didn't Daddy. I didn't. Even though she is now my
mistress. (*Pause.*) You see, what happened was well about a
month ago I went around to see her, and the door was open,
on the latch, so I knew she was expecting me, and so I went in.
And there she was. On the sofa. And a strange noise coming
from upstairs. Rather alarming, actually, until I realized it was
just the little girl asleep, snoring — and the boys were out,
doing something hideous I suppose, anyway they weren't doing
it inside — they like to catch cats, you know, and tie plastic
bags around their heads. So. So it was just her. On the sofa.
Looking so defeated and — and hopeless — and the snoring
from above. And me. And she said, oh doctor, oh doctor. She's
— she's Irish you know. And started to cry. So I went over to
her. And she seemed to want, to expect — to *need* me to — and
— well — anyway — I did. You see, it was something I could do,
something I could give her, there being so little one can give
even those who love one, isn't that true, Daddy, and here was
something so simple, I've always found it so easy to, well — and
there's always been something about her that touched me you
see — and — and afterwards she clung to me as if — and I
cuddled her and everything was — I like to think it was peaceful
for a little time, Carla snoring safely away still, the boys still
out and a man holding her — it wasn't sex, you see, not for her
either — (*pause*) I prescribed myself, if you like. On the
National Health. Anyhow that's how I tried to look at it.
(*Laughs.*) As I say holding her. (*Little pause.*) I didn't feel
guilty or ashamed, or embarrassed. Not at all. In fact afterwards
I used her little shower thing in the kitchen — she's very clean,
by the way, and neat and house-proud — pathetically so really
— again I don't know quite why I told Marianne that — you
know, the squalor — and I massaged the back of her neck,

where she gets pain, and looked in on Carla, and discussed an
operation on her adenoids and then went home as if I — as if
for once I'd been an effective doctor. You see. And I made
love to Marianne that night as usual. Or rather she made love
to me as she could see I was tired. (*Smiles. Pause.*) But of
course nothing ends — nothing like that ends with the act,
does it? Why should it? Give someone valium for much needed
calm and in no time they're desperate for their calming valium,
and it's no good explaining to them — every doctor knows that
these days — I mean, well what I'm trying to say is that simply
that I um, that I — anyway it's all more complicated than that,
because after all I didn't not want to, I have to admit it, even
though I didn't positively want to, and wouldn't have if she
hadn't moved me to it, for her sake and not for mine, but on
the other hand her face and my heart — so not like valium at all
really. (*Laughs.*) Now she looks upon me as her lover. Her man.
She's as possessive of me as — well, she feels she has a right to
me, as she's given me her body, as she puts it. She is Irish, after
all. And so in return she thinks she's entitled to something from
me — oh, not just money, other than the odd pound here and
there, and who can blame her for that? But well, more of *me*.
My time. My attention. My love. And now she's taken, poor
soul, to threatening me. (*Pause.*) I have a feeling she's told her
brutes of boys. Or perhaps they've watched. Or she's allowed
them to watch — no, no, I'm sure that's unfair, unworthy — it's
just that there's a window and once I thought I — oh, I don't
know. It doesn't really matter, does it? But if I don't go around
then they come around, to the surgery — and this morning, of
course, to the house — so — so — it'll get worse, especially now
she's becoming so much more robust, taking so much more
interest in — in life. I've tried to think it through — right to the
worst end — the scandal, and I'll be struck off, I suppose, and
then what it'll mean for old Marianne and the children — one
day — and — and — then I've tried to put it in the larger scheme,
sub specie aeternitas, no *aeternitatis* sorry Daddy (*a little laugh*)
well, who's to decide between our deserts, Marianne's and mine,
on the one hand, and Mrs O'Killiam's on the other, we don't
deserve more than she does, do we, and we've already had more,
far more — and then it struck me, you see. The real thing. That
I didn't care. I'd even quite welcome it. Because once you do

begin to look at it *sub specie* it's really all such a pitiful
charade, isn't it, or perhaps not even pitiful, merely a charade,
with none of it mattering at all in view of what happens all
over the world, every minute of the day, and when one thinks
it through that far — no, no, when *I'd* thought it through that
far I felt a tremendous relief, you see, because then I could
face the fact — the fact that I've never cared, never, I've always
really known that nothing matters, and I remembered the
night Dick was killed — when I left you that night and went
home and sat it the kitchen, the house was breathing you know,
with life, Marianne upstairs waiting for me, children in all the
rooms, another in Marianne's womb — and Mrs O'Killiam in
her loneliness also, as it's turned out, waiting for me — and
some poor devil who'd lost his eye and his daughter in a car
crash I'd been to see — and Dick dead, Dick, and I didn't care,
not about any of us, not about Marianne or Tom or Piers or
Nigel or Simon or Nindy or the unborn or any of the Mrs
O'Killiams anywhere or you here mourning the only one of us
you loved — and so I gave myself a couple of jolly hard punches,
Daddy, right in the face, to make myself care about something
— and then old Marianne came down, poor old Marianne, and
I looked at her and thought, no, no, I don't care about you
either, poor old girl, and now there's Nanty with a brain
tumour more than likely so you see, Daddy, so you see, what
is the point, the point of caring for each other and loving each
other when the end is always and always the same, *sub specie*
or any way you look at it, Daddy, do *you* know by any chance,
God given chance? (*Pause.*) Do you? And if you don't why did
you bring us into the world, how did you dare — how did you
— I'm sorry. I'm sorry to be so childish. I should probably have
asked that question all those years ago, when you were telling
us about *hubris*, but if you can answer now I'd be jolly
grateful. So I'll know what to say to my lot when the time
comes. Can you, Daddy? (*Laughs, stares desperately at*
JASPER.)

MARGARET *enters from left.*

There is a pause.

MARGARET. Sorry.   Am I interrupting?

HENRY. What? Oh good Heavens no, Daddy and I were just having one of our jaws, weren't we Daddy?

MARGARET *lights a cigarette. Her hand is trembling.*

HENRY. I gather you and Marianne had a bit of a ding-dong, I hope you didn't take it too — too — I know she didn't.

MARGARET. Look, the thing is, I've got to get back to London soon.

HENRY. Oh. What a pity.

MARGARET. And I've just looked in on Ben.

HENRY. Ah. Yes. How is he? I'm afraid he might have had a spot too much, we were reminiscing, you know what it's like when we haven't seen each other for a bit, eh Daddy? (*Laughs.*)

MARGARET. He's sprawled across the bed of his childhood, with his thumb in his mouth. He's making little mewling sounds at the back of his throat. He's dribbling. And he stinks of scotch.

HENRY. Oh. Well um —

MARGARET. So I gather he's been through his fit and frenzy stage, has he?

HENRY. Well. Well, perhaps he did become a little — I'm sorry, Maggie.

MARGARET. I'm not, I'm afraid. He was due for another bout, and I wanted him to have it here. I'm returning him, you see. Giving him back. Sorry. That's unnecessarily brutal. But I've had quite enough of him, and I need you to keep him here, please, until I've moved myself out of the flat and found a place where I'll be safe. Actually, my publishers have already set that side of things in motion. (*Pause.*) No doubt you think I'm being very hard. Yes. But the last few years have been a nightmare. Besides, I'm not Ben's wife anymore. Let alone his nurse, surrogate mother, victim and tart on demand. I'm a novelist. My first novel taught me that much. Whatever *you* think of it. And now that I've begun a new one, I'm going to need all my wits and as much peace as I can manage. Along with the usual ration of luck and inspiration. You see. I'm sorry. I *am* sorry to take advantage. But then you *are* a doctor, aren't you, so you'll know what to do. And as you're also a

decent man and a loving brother I'm fairly sure you'll do it.
Oh, and there's something I should tell you. As far as I can
establish, his Vintross doesn't exist. At least the only Vintross
I can trace is a car-park attendant at the B.B.C. And I don't
know if he got on to Hugh Rhys Jones, but if he did, Hugh
Rhys Jones didn't stab himself to death in a Chinese restaurant
or whatever. He's merely been transferred to Cardiff. Which
may amount to the same thing, of course. (*Gets up.*) I've heard
there's a good clinic outside Staines. I'll get my publisher to
send you its address. And of course any committal papers you
want me to sign. Oh — and my apologies to Marianne — explain
that I was a trifle on edge. And now I'd better get away before
he makes one of his spectral recoveries. They can be rather
unnerving. Goodbye. (*Turns left to go out.*)

BENEDICT *enters from left. He is trembling. His colour is
ghastly. He walks slowly to* MARGARET. *Stands in front of
her.*

HENRY (*gets up*). Ben —

BENEDICT. It was Dick, of course. Wasn't it? Yes, it was Dick.
He's just come back you see and told me so. Back, Henry,
Daddy. Just as he used to be, twenty-five years ago. And he
was wearing that smile, you'd know the smile, Henry, when
we'd caught him out in one of his little meannesses, his
stealings, and he'd decided to make it up. And then — then
Daddy — he put his hand out, towards me, as if he was going
to touch me. And I said, 'Dick, Dick — ' and he turned and
went. Went away from me.

HENRY. Ben — old Ben — it wasn't Dick —

BENEDICT. Yes, it was Hen. It was, Daddy. Because then she
came, you see. Didn't you darling. I could sense you above me,
when I was lying there thinking about Dick. You thought I was
asleep, didn't you darling, but I could sense you looking down
at me, triumphant. Isn't that right, darling? Triumphant. And
then you went away. But I understood, I understood what it
was old Dick, our old Dick, Henry, had come back to tell me,
Daddy. What was it like to have Dick's willy inside of you,
darling? Did he hold you against the dark, as I did. Did he?
(*Smiles pathetically.*)

JENNY enters through the french windows.

JENNY. I take it he's not come back, then?

HENRY. Oh. Well actually I think Ben saw him a short while ago. Didn't you Ben?

BENEDICT. What?

HENRY. He came into your room for a moment, you were just telling us. Because that's where he's staying the night, you see. Matthew.

BENEDICT. Matthew?

HENRY. Yes, Ben. Matthew, old chap. (*Goes to him gently, takes his arm.*) Matthew, you see.

BENEDICT. Oh. Oh yes Matthew — so alike, so alike it makes the heart — heart — sorry Hen, sorry — sorry — darling. Sorry Jen, sorry Daddy.

JENNY. Did he say anything?

HENRY. No, apparently he came in and saw — well, old Ben was having a nap, weren't you Ben, so he went away again, apparently, from what Ben was saying, didn't he, eh Ben?

JENNY. Well, that's our day together. He has to be back first thing tomorrow. Our only day together in a month and then another month until half term, and I can't go on looking for him any more, I'm soaked through, my feet are wet and I'm worn out, he's quite worn me out with his — of course you realize it's deliberate, don't you, I expect you've all noticed how he avoids me, when I so much as put my hand on his arm he flinches, draws away from me — he loathes my touch, you see, his mother's touch. Oh yes — yes — I'm sure you've noticed — perhaps you want it even, do you? So that you can see he's still Dick's son, not mine, I expect that's why you wanted him to stay on at that school after Dick's death — well, I'll tell you one thing, he's not going back, no, he's not going back there, with that housemaster — I hate that housemaster — so snide and knowing, as if he knows things about my own son that I don't, and writing to you, how dare he write to you! How dare you let him! (*To* HENRY.) Well he won't any more, you won't any more, he's coming back home with me, to live with me where I can watch him and guard him and look after him, I've a right to that, if I'm going to die for him a thousand times a day I've a right to that, I'm not going to let him end up like Dick, no I'm not, we're never going to set foot in this house again — neither of us! Neither of us! He's *my* son. Not *yours*! (*Looks around at them.*) Yes, this is Dick's frump speaking. Dick's frump! That's what you all thought of me as, you couldn't understand how your brilliant Dick could come to marry me, could you — but then you didn't know him, didn't see him as I saw him, night after night, crying, or curled up — so pathetic — I did my best, held him and cuddled him, but I knew it was hopeless, hopeless, nobody could have saved him, nobody, every time he went off on that motor-bike I knew — knew what he wanted and at the end I almost wanted it too, yes I did, because if he couldn't find anything in me or our Matthew to keep him then he might as well — well I'm not letting him go like that, not letting my Matthew go like that. I'm not. I'm not.

MARGARET (*goes to her*). Jenny — Jenny — I know what you're feeling —

JENNY (*slaps her*). Do you? (*Laughs.*) Do you? With your nasty mean little novel, do you think — do you think he cared for you either, why, why you were one of hundreds, hundreds, why there was an Australian sociologist at the same time as you, the very same time, she was called Dick's Kangaroo because she'd hop into bed with him anywhere, even places where there wasn't one, that was the joke about her, and his students, Dick's lucky dips, and that furry little woman in the bursar's office, all going on at the same time, he couldn't wait to be shot of you, give you the bum's rush or old heave-ho he called it, that's why he started you off on your writing, so you'd leave him alone, God he would have laughed to see you smirking away on television, and — and — do you think it mattered, mattered to me, monopoly, ping-pong, Agatha Christie, sordid little affairs with people like you, anything — anything to keep it at bay —

MATTHEW *enters through the french windows.*

There is a pause.

MATTHEW. Um — (*clears his throat*) oh you're here then?

MARIANNE (*enters through the arch.*) Ah, all here, jolly good — Nanty's seeing them around to the van, darling, and I've just potted Nindy but no luck this time, even Gramps's magic didn't work, you must have spent her last penny after lunch, eh Gramps, anyway we're all set darling, sorry we've got to leave so early, old Henry's fault for being needed as usual, but golly it was lovely seeing us all together again, eh Gramps?

DAISY (*enters from left*). I've got them all in dears, now Nindy's got the pottie and Nigel's looking after the boots and Simon and Nigel are in charge of the coats and Tom's promised not to toot the horn, but before you go dears there's something you want to tell them, isn't there Jasper, I've been thinking dear, and they have a right to know who I am, haven't they dear. We're married, you see. Jasper and I. (*Pause.*) Aren't we Jasper. There! (*Laughs.*) We knew that would surprise you. Didn't we Jasper?

There is a pause.

Oh, it wasn't a proper ceremony, in church and in white, with bridesmaids and bouquets or anything like that, no no, it was just a thing in an office, the most ordinary thing in the world except for a sweet old lady who played the organ, didn't she Jasper, but it was all a bit of a rush, you know, people waiting in the waiting room, and leaving as we entered, weren't there Jasper, but they have to keep at it all the time, you know — quite a little business in its way but Jasper was, well you know how he feels things, always so quick, isn't he dear? His shoulders shook and his mouth trembled, it did you know! And so distinguished with his white mane and a carnation in his button and he even cried, didn't you Jasper, and he was so ashamed because he thought he was holding them up you see — with so many to come, and probably queues forming — but I said, I told him, they're used to it you know, people crying and overcome and behaving strangely, they allow for it dear, they take it into account, they'll fit everybody in so don't you worry, and sure enough it just swung open, the door on the other side you see, not where we'd come in, but on the other side — oh so well organized — and out we went, didn't

we Jasper, out we went! And the people who'd been before us
were still on the pavement, laughing and chattering weren't
they dear and clambering into their cars, and another car
arrived, didn't it Jasper, with a new lot you see just as I said,
and then our car came up, we'd hired it especially, oh so grand
it was, shiny and black to take us home, and home we came,
didn't we Jasper, and I said as we went, there there my love,
my sweet, my darling — it's all over, it's finished, wasn't it easy
and quick, all finished at last and he said 'Rose, Rose — ' aaaah!
— and I said ' No no Jasper, I'm not your Rose my dear, I'm
your Daisy dear', and 'Oh my dear Daisy' he said, so sweet he
was — 'Oh my dear Daisy, not over, my Daisy, but beginning
my love', he was tired you see, weren't you Jasper, quite dead
you were, weren't you my dear, we'll have children he said, to
keep us going, send them forth in life, didn't you Jasper, think
of them waiting, waiting to enter, we'll bring them forth, for
life awaits them, the door will open, we'll send them towards
it — didn't you love, aaah aaaah my darling — the door will
open, we'll send them towards it —

*During this speech and the following speeches the room is
brightening — through natural sunlight after the rain to an
unnatural brightness.*

The door will open, we'll send them towards it — the door is
open —

THE REST (*except* JASPER). We'll send them towards it.

   JASPER *is struggling, as if to rise. His eyes fixed in wonder.*

DAISY. The door will open —

THE REST (*except* JASPER). We'll send them towards it.

DAISY. The door is open —

THE REST (*except* JASPER). We've sent them towards it!
DAISY &
THE REST. The door is open, we'll send them towards it,
   the door is open, we've sent them towards it,
   the door is open, we'll send them towards it,
   the door is open, we've sent them towards it —

   JASPER *has almost made it to his feet.*

The door is open, the door is open, the door is open!

Stillness.

A prolonged honking of the horn.

JASPER *subsides into his chair.*

DAISY. Oh really — I did tell him not to!

HENRY. Sorry Nanty, but it's hard to resist —

MARIANNE. — Anyway Nanty, we are just off, this second, don't worry — well Jenny — (*kisses her*) and Margaret (*coolly*) and Ben (*kissing them both*) I hope it won't be so long next time because Gramps does love it when you — and old Mat — see you next hols, eh —

HENRY (*meanwhile*). Ben, you um, well we'll be in touch and — and Maggie — um, um, take care the two of you um (*putting a hand on* BENEDICT's *shoulder, kissing* MARGARET) and Jenny my dear, now you're not to worry, everything'll be — and Mat — keep up the good work!

DAISY (*throughout this*). — aaah, what a shame you couldn't stay for tea, it was all laid you know, especially, but everything's in, don't worry, Nindy, the pottie, Nigel and Tom the boots and coats — so that's all right — nothing forgotten this time —

HENRY. And Nanty — (*kisses her*) I shan't forget about the headaches, I'll see to that straight away —

DAISY. Oh thank you dear, so sweet, and I'll keep on with the moist pads, shan't I Jasper?

MARIANNE (*kissing her*). I hope we weren't too much for you this time —

DAISY. What, no no, of course not dear — they were no trouble, the boys and little Nindy — aaah! — You're never any trouble, are they Jasper?

Honking off.

MARIANNE. Well darling, mustn't keep Mrs O'Killiam waiting!

HENRY. Golly no, well God bless, God bless — and see you Daddy, as usual.

MARIANNE. Yes God Bless Gramps — see you as usual.

HENRY and MARIANNE *go out left to the accompaniment of honking.*

The honking stops.

DAISY. Oooh — you see it starts my head off — well, there we are, at least we can have a proper grown-up tea, we adore the little ones, don't we Jasper — but I must say they make it difficult to have a proper grown-up — but I've kept most of the rock-cakes for you, Matthew, I know Jenny got them for you specially so I only allowed them. half each so you can have a good tuck-in dear, but oh that reminds me I still haven't settled — now how much did we say it was Jenny, fifty-six p. but of course my purse, I still haven't found, did I ask you if you'd seen it Matthew, have you seen it dear, my purse, small, green, in velours —

MATTHEW (*with sudden fluency*). Your purse, gosh no Nanty, I haven't seen any purse at all, a small green one did you say in — well I'll certainly keep an eye out for it, it's terrible when one loses things, I do it all the time don't I Mummy, I hope there wasn't any money or anything valuable in it.

DAISY. Well about four pounds 85p. but it must be here somewhere, you see it's the purse, that's what I care about, it was a present from Jasper, years ago, wasn't it Jasper?

JENNY (*who was watching* MATTHEW *during his speech*). Ready for our walk, darling?

MATTHEW. Oh um well I um —

DAISY. What, walk, but what about your tea, aren't you going to have our tea first?

JENNY. No, I'd like to go now.

MATTHEW. Oh well um — (*laughs*) I'll just go and get my — my um —

JENNY. You won't need it. Whatever it is. So let's go straight away darling and together if you please — (*goes over, takes him by the hand, tightly*) so that we can't lose each other, the front way or the back, whichever you prefer.

MATTHEW. Oh um well let's go — well, I don't mind.

JENNY. This way then. (*Leads him to door left, then has to let go*

*of his hand. Stands aside to let him pass. Follows closely,
shutting the door behind her.*)

DAISY. Oh well I must say — you'd have thought they'd have
waited, wouldn't you Jasper, they could have had tea first as
they're always so hungry —

BENEDICT (*during this, has gone over to* MARGARET, *has stood
staring directly into her eyes*). Ready, darling?

MARGARET. What for, darling?

BENEDICT. Why home, of course.

MARGARET. But this is your home.

BENEDICT. Not any more, darling. My home is our flat, with the
study in it that I painted for you. In pastel colours. And you
know, darling, I'm rather anxious to get back to it. To give
Vintross a ring. He'll want to know how things are. And you
must want to get back, too. I know what it's like now — when
you start a new one. (*Little pause.*) Coming? (*Little pause.*)
Coming, darling?

DAISY. What, what do you mean — you're not going too — but
the tea's out you know — or Benedict a drink, dear — you
always like a drink before you go.

BENEDICT. Oh no, Nanty — (*leading* MARGARET *towards the
french windows.*) I've given that stuff up now virtually for
good, haven't I Daddy — but we'll be back soon — We won't
leave it so long before the next time, Daddy, that's a promise,
isn't it, darling? (*They go.*)

DAISY. What, well that's all very well but after all the trouble I
went to — and the muffins — all those muffins — and what for?
What for? Lay it down on the assumption and then just clear
it all away again — you see — like a house-keeper — but what
about you, Jasper, how do you feel, are you all right dear,
you've gone very quiet all of a sudden.

JASPER *makes a slight noise.*

DAISY. What, dear?

JASPER. The door is open!

DAISY. Dear?

JASPER. The door is open!

DAISY. Oh, you're feeling the chill again, and such a warm sunny evening now that it's rained, but of course if you're feeling the chill, I know how it goes right through you, right through your whole system — (*going to the french windows, shutting them, locking them*) there — is that better — and oh the light — we don't need the light any more now that it's light (*turns off lights*) — and my headache you know, much better now that everybody's — (*collecting the scotch bottle and glass*) not that we don't like having them of course — though they might have stayed for tea — (*as she goes out through the arch*) don't we, dear?

The lights continue to go down steadily, until only JASPER *in his chair is lit. That light remains for a few seconds and then as it goes down, the sound of organ music, distantly, then swelling to fill the theatre as*

Curtain